Arabian Horses
"Poetry in Motion"
For Kids

Nature Books for Kids
By
K. Bennett

JD-Biz Publishing

Read More Amazing Animal Books

Purchase at Amazon.com

Table of Contents

Introduction

Introduction

*A good horse makes short miles. ~ **George Elliot***

***

Arabian Horses: The Arabian horse or Arab horse is a beautiful breed with a shiny coat! They are very fast and strong, and can ride around for a very long time without getting tired!

These amazing horses come from the Arabian Peninsula. Do you remember what a peninsula is?

What is a Peninsula?

The dictionary describes a Peninsula as: '*A piece of land almost surrounded by water or "coming" out of a body of water.*' So, its land with lots of water around it!

The Arabian Peninsula is found in the continent of Asia, and is the biggest one in the world!

Use your imagination to fly to the edge of the Peninsula. What do you see around you?

Look to the west and southwest to find the Red Sea. Can you see it? What does it look like?

Then look to the south to find the Arabian Sea. Is it big or small?

Now look to the east and you will find the Persian Gulf and the Gulf of Oman. What color is the water?

Are you lost? Not to worry. Ask your parent on a guardian to help you find the locations on a map, and you will see where Arabian horses come from!

What makes the Arabian horse so special?

Arabian horses really look good! Do you agree with me? They have a nice, well-shaped head and carry their tail in a special way! Because of their unique looks, many people recognize Arabian horses when they see them.

For thousands of years Arabian horses were used to make other horses better. Do you remember what **crossbreeding** is all about? In all of our other horse books, we mentioned what this means:

The dictionary at Kids.Net.Au says the word "Crossbreeding" means this: *"(genetics) the act of mixing different species or varieties of animals or plants and thus to produce hybrids."*

So they mixed the horses together — using the Arabian horse breed — to make much better horses.

Arabian horses were used so much, that most modern horses have a little Arabian DNA!

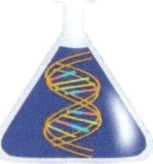

Arabian horses are really smart and very versatile. This means they are very good in many different areas. And they are found all around the world, in places like the United States, Australia, Continental Europe, South America and the Middle East. And today, they are used in many different "equestrian" activities and challenges like endurance riding and trail riding. And guess what? They are very good at it!

With their high spirit, patience and beautiful personality, Arabian horses are an amazing part of nature's magnificent wonders.

Enjoy learning more about them!

Arabian horses

WOULD YOU LIKE TO DRAW A SIMPLE HORSE? LEARN HERE!

Howtodrawanimals.net has a simple 8 step tutorial on drawing horses. I thought you might like to try!

1- ***FIRST:*** Before you search online, please get a parent's or guardian's permission!

2- In your browser (Chrome, Internet explorer, Firefox, Torch) type: http://www.howtodrawanimals.net/how-to-draw-a-horse

3 – Then follow the steps.

*If this tutorial is too difficult for you or if you don't like it, then try the **Wikihow** tutorial instead:*

1- In your browser (Chrome, Internet explorer, Firefox, Torch) type: www.Wikihow.com

3- In the search box at the top of the page type: *Draw a simple horse*. Once the search is complete, you should see a title that reads: "**How to draw a simple horse: 11 steps with pictures**."

4 – Click on the link and follow the steps.

5- Have fun!

Arabian horses

Chapter 1

Nice to meet you!

History: Arabian horses have a rich history that goes back many, many years. Some say as far back as **4,500 – 5,000** years! That is a very long time, don't you think?

How do scientists know Arabian horses were around so long ago? Because Archeology has found some horses that look a lot like the Arabian horses we know today!

For example, in Libya, they found rock paintings more than 8,000 years old. Guess what was painted on the rock walls? Yes! Horses that look a lot like the Arabian breed.

You might think of it as old pictures from the past, showing us the future. And this teaches us a few important things about the Arabian horse. Think about this:

Arabian horses come from the desert. So this gives you an idea of what kind of climate they live in!

The Bedouins loved their horses and treated them as a proud member of the family, and not just a common animal!

Many times Arabian horses slept inside the tents with their masters. This was to give them a good shelter and protect them from thieves!

When Arabians were bred, they were chosen for their good personality and easy working style. This blend of personality and strength produced a horse that was…

~Eager to please
~Happy to obey
~Sensitive
~Intelligent
~Good-natured and a
~Strong worker.

What a great horse!

Expanding horizons

The Arabian horse came to Europe during the 7th century. What happened? The Moors invaded Spain. Do you know who the Moors were?

The Moors came from Morocco and entered the Iberian Peninsula, 'Andalus.' During those years, specifically 711 AD, the moors had a great impact on European culture. Studies like: Astronomy, Math, Chemistry, Physics and Philosophy spread everywhere! But guess what else the Moors brought with them? Did you guess? Yes! They brought Arabian horses.

A scholar of the time wrote about the conquest like this…

~The reins of their (Moors) horses were as fire, their faces black as pitch, their eyes shone like burning candles, their horses were swift as leopards and the riders fiercer than a wolf in a sheepfold at night …

(Source: **Blackhistorystudies.com**)

Can you imagine a horse with reigns that look like fire? Picture it in your mind. Now, imagine this same horse with fiery reigns running straight towards you like a leopard, covering the ground with super-fast speeds…How do you think you might feel?

DIG DEEPER!

Would you like to know how the Moors helped Europeans to learn about Science? Research the information at your library, school or online.

Remember: Before you search (If you are a minor), please get a parent's or guardian's permission!

Arabian horses

Beautiful coat

Characteristics: Arabians horses are very unique horses in size and shape. How so? Let's start with the basics and we will expand to the other amazing parts of this beautiful horse.

Size: Approximately 14.1 to 15.2 hands and over.

Weight: The Arab horse can weigh 800 to 1000 pounds. Of course, this does not mean some can't weigh a bit less or more, but this is the standard weight.

Coats: Arabian horses have shiny coats in bright shades of brown, black, bay, chestnut and a roan-like pattern. There are other color variations too including white markings on their face and legs.

Do you remember what *Roan* is?

Roan: This is not just one color. It is a pattern of colors with a mixture of white. The horse will have lots of white hairs mixed with their other hairs. Usually the head, lower legs, mane and tail are more solid or will have fewer white hairs. Sometimes, this color variation is called Silvery like the moonlight!

And now for the fun part! What makes the Arab horse really unique?

Arabian horses have 17 ribs, 5 Lumbar bones and 16 tail vertebrae. Most other horses have 18 ribs, 6 Lumbar bones and 18 tail vertebrae. You might say…so what? Well, these changes give the Arabian horse a really cute head – usually called a 'dish face', a special shaped tail, fine bones and a nice shaped back!

This is called the: ***Skeletal structure.***

Feels good to run!

DIG DEEPER!

The Emperor Napoleon I of France rode a horse called **Marengo**. Do you know what color Marengo was? Find out by doing more research!

FUN FACTS FOR KIDS:
Measuring horses: What is **HANDS**?

This is a neat way to measure horses. The measurement refers to hands, literal hands! The symbol is usually HH (Hands high). So you would say 15hh, 16hh or 17hh. This means 15 hands, 16 hands and 17 hands. You might be wondering why people measure horses in hands?

Well, many years ago people did not have rulers or measuring sticks like we do today. So they used whatever they had…and they had hands. So horses are measured like this. You can do it too! How?

Think about it like this: One hand is 4 inches.

So if a horse is 15 hands multiply this by 4. (15 x 4) and you will get 60 inches. And if a horse is 16 hands multiply this number by 4. (16 x 4) and you will get 64 inches.

Now that you know how to do it, you can measure other horses for yourself!

Arabian horses

Feels good in the snow!

Events: Arabians stand out in many different types of events, and one of them is endurance riding. In our book: "*Canadian Horses for Kids,*" we wrote about this event but I will repeat it again for you!

Endurance riding: This type of event depends on the distance, trail and terrain. This simply means what the land looks like, if it has hills, curving snakelike roads, lots of rocks and things like that.

Some of the competitive events are 25 miles long all the way to 100 miles! Do you think you could ride your horse for 100 miles? I don't think I can do that!

Sometimes it does not matter which horse passes the finish line. What matters is how long it takes to ride that far. Sounds complicated? I think I would much rather ride for fun! What about you?

Arabians also excel in dressage. Can you imagine their beautiful, elegant strides eating up the ground and making the judges go wild? Do you remember what dressage is?

Dressage: Dressage has been around for a very long time. The USDF (United States Dressage Federation) organization talks about five different levels.

~Training level
~First level
~Second level
~Third level
~Fourth level

Before you begin this type of training, there are several things to have to do. *Wikihow.com* suggests the following steps.

1- Both you and your horse need to know each other very well! And you need to know if you can trust each other. So a close relationship is very important before any training can begin! This is where Arabian horses excel. Remember they are eager to please you, so they will be happy to work along with you. They are smart too so they learn quickly!

2- You have to start to work on the way your horse walks or trots. This is referred to as a **gait**. It is very important for your horse to walk in the right way. Arabians have a beautiful **gait,** so this makes it easy for them to participate.

3- **Transitions:** This is when you want your horse to change from one movement to another. It is important to do this in a smooth manner. It should be just like putting one footstep in front of the other without tripping over your feet!

4- Your position in the saddle should look comfortable and balanced. And your heels should be down at all times.

5 – Practice makes perfect. To get good at any skill, you need to do it over and over again. Practicing with your horse is a great way to get good at riding him!

The flowers smell nice!

Arabian horses have done a lot for the horses we know today. Almost every "light" breed of horse that exists, owes its heritage to the Arab horse.

Here are a few reasons why we can thank the Arabian horse for a job well done!

~Arabian horses have helped many rulers to win wars!

~They have helped many children to appreciate how wonderful it is to own a horse that wants to make you happy!

~Arabian horses live for a long time and work very hard for their owners.

~Even if an Arabian horse is old, it is a great first time horse for the entire family!

(Source: ***horses.about.com***)

DIG DEEPER!

How did Arabian horses come to the United States? Look up a man by the name of Nathan Harrison of Virginia. How did he play a part in history? *Hint:* The year was 1725.

Water tastes good!

Care: Arabian horses are very sensitive so they don't like to be cooped up in a small stall. They are much too smart and will get bored quickly. Imagine what an intelligent, bored horse can get into when you have him in a small space! Lots of trouble, right? Try to give them lots of open spaces to expend their energy and stretch their beautiful long legs!

Keeping them with other horses is a great way to help your Arab horse feel happy. Add some toys too like traffic cones and balls for even more fun!

Living: Arabians take a longer time to reach adulthood than other horses. If you aren't careful, they can get hurt if you are too rough with them. So don't do crazy riding and jumping before they are old enough! Usually, they reach adulthood when they are 5 years old.

Fresh air is great!

Children & Beginners: Arabian horses can get a little over happy at times! And sometimes they have a lot of energy to use up, so this may not be the best ride for children and beginners. Get an older Arabian horse instead. This will be a much better choice for younger ones and those who are just starting to ride!

Chapter 2

Out for a small trot!

Have you learned anything new about the Arab horse? Wonderful!
Now, we will detail the steps for training all horses and then give you
some interesting facts about Arabian horses! Are you ready?

Training: *Wikihow.com* recommends the following steps to train horses:

1-***First of all, don't scare the horse***. That means you should not run up
or sneak up on them suddenly. This is not a hard to understand. Do you

like it when people run or sneak up on you suddenly? It may scare you when someone does that, right? Then a horse will feel the same way.

2-**Be gentle and talk kindly to your horse**. There is no need to yell, shout or talk harshly to your horse. Again, this idea is not hard to understand. Do you like it when people talk to you gently? Or do you want them to shout and yell at you? Isn't it nicer to treat others kindly and don't you appreciate it when others do the same for you? Your Arabian horse will appreciate your kind manner too!

Out with friends!

3-**Most horses love to be touched**. Show them your feelings through your hands. Stroke them on the head, massage their neck, hug them, brush them and communicate your affection through kind fingers. Imagine how happy your horse will be!

4-**Try to spend as much time as you can with your horse**. In any friendship, regular visits are the key! No matter what you have to do, stop by and visit your horse just to remind them that you're around. They will be so happy to see you and the more you spend time with them, the stronger your bond will grow.

5- **A nice reward**. A tasty treat, rub or pat down, yummy food, grooming of whatever other treat you might have in mind, will be a great idea! Do this at the end of the day to let your horse know how much you enjoyed spending time with them.

Arabian horses

GENERAL HORSE TIPS FOR KIDS:

Arabian horses need lots of attention and loving care. But if you don't have an Arabian horse, does this mean you won't care as much for your other horse? Not at all! Here are some tips you can think about. These basic principles apply to most if not all horses. Are you ready?

-Your horse's diet is very important. Some horses have very hot blood and some have cooler blood. If your horse is hot blooded, they will need less protein in their diet.

-Learn how to properly discipline your horse. ***Remember:*** These animals are very sensitive and Arabian horses can get hurt if discipline is done in the wrong way. You might need to get professional advice if you don't know what to do.

-Horses love to get tender rubs and soft pats. Things like rubbing their ears, nose, eyes and mouth is great. And a massage is even better!

Arabian horses

-If a horse is trained really well, he or she will invite YOU for a ride. You should be looking for the invitation! Then you will enjoy an awesome time!

-Your horse can sense your moods and behavior. If you are confident your horse will be confident too!

-You should feed your horse from a bucket and not your hand. (This is the recommendation, but I feel it is better to feed them with your hand from time to time! It seems to generate more trust and respect, but that is just my humble opinion on the subject. What do you think?)

(Source: Frank Bell- *Horsewhisperer.com*)

With these tips in mind, you will have a happy, confident and loving Arabian horse!

Where is my treat?

Chapter 3

As promised, here are some interesting facts about Arabian horses you may like to know. Share them with your parents or with your classmates if you like!

~Arabian horses have many beautiful colors and shiny coats, but underneath their coat, they have black skin! Why? Many feel it is because they come from the desert and black skin helped to protect them from the burning sun.

~The movie: "The Black Stallion" starred Mickey Rooney and a magnificent black Arabian stallion named: Cass Ole. How did he do in his acting role?

~Arabian horses can be very loyal if…and this is important… if you treat them well. If you don't treat them nicely, they will be hard to handle!

~The Bedouin tribes used the Arab horse to travel very far over the desert. This was the best horse to use because they have large lungs and can endure long distances.

~Arabian horses are the oldest purebred horse in the world! That's pretty amazing, don't you think?

(Source: *Qatarliving.com*)

~Arabian horses pass on beautiful characteristics to their children! This is one reason why breeders love them so much.

INTERESTING HORSE FUN FACTS FOR KIDS:

- Horses are great at listening! They can turn their ears in different ways to improve their hearing. If you whisper and say something bad about your horse, they just might hear you!

-Horses are the best sleepers on the planet. They can sleep lying down and standing up! Can you do that?

- Horses are herbivores. Do you know that this means? It means they eat plants or are plant eaters, if you like this term better.

-Horses have feelings and emotions too! Treat them kindly with lots of patience and love. You may be surprised at the results!

-After a horse is born in just a few hours it can run away from you!

-There was a horse that lived many years ago called "Old Billy," also called Billy Boy or Billy. Guess how long he lived? 62 years! Wow, isn't that amazing?

(Source: ***Onekind.org & Sciencekids.co.nz***)

DIG DEEPER!

General Ulysses S. Grant got two friends by the names of Leopard and Lindentree. Who were they and what did they have to do with Arabian horses? Dig deeper and find out!

Arabian horses

Conclusion:

Best friends always

In conclusion: Horses are beautiful creatures, and Arabian horses are one of the most beautiful creatures on this planet! They are strong, gentle and very intelligent equines. They are also loyal and willing to please you.

This is a great time to learn a bit more about these noble animals. For example, did you know famous men like Genghis Khan, Alexander the Great and George Washington rode Arabian horses? What were their horses like? What about their coat colors?

After your research, you may be amazed at what you can discover. And if you don't know exactly what to research about Arabians…Choose some part of the horse you really like (It can be the tail, mane, ears, body, size, personality, history, etc) and learn a bit more about that subject.

Something you can research is the special bond Arab horses have with their owners. What is their secret? What makes them so special in this way?

Another option is this: If you are in school and participate in show and tell or a science fair, use the Arabian Stallion as your subject. Many of your classmates may have heard of Arabian horses, but they may not know how important it has been to other horses over the years. And it would be nice to share what you find with others.

I hope you have enjoyed our series on horses! It is our sincere wish that you continue to learn and expand your horizons. After all…who knows what wonderful things are out there…just waiting for you to find it!

"Educating the mind without educating the heart is no education at all." - *Aristotle*

Author Bio

K. Bennett loves to write for both children and adults. Many different subjects are interesting to develop, but writing for children is special to her heart.

Her favorite pastimes include reading, traveling and discovering new things. Each of these activities helps to fuel her imagination and acts like a blank canvas waiting for more stories.

She is intrigued with fantasy elements like hidden worlds and faraway lands. Basically anything that gets her imagination soaring to new heights!

Her writing credits include children books online, short stories for online magazines, and two novellas listed at Amazon.com

Our books are available at

1. Amazon.com

2. Barnes and Noble

3. Itunes

4. Kobo

5. Smashwords

6. Google Play Books

Arabian horses

This book is published by

JD-Biz Corp

P O Box 374

Mendon, Utah 84325

http://www.jd-biz.com/

Read more books from John Davidson

Amazon.com Author Link

Arabian horses

Arabian horses

www.ingramcontent.com/pod-product-compliance
Lightning Source LLC
Chambersburg PA
CBHW050919290526
45792CB00002B/816